Katie's butterfly

Story by Jenny Giles

Illustrations by Meredith Thomas

Katie went into the school yard, and ran to meet her friend Anna.

"Katie!" shouted Anna. "Your butterfly has come out of its chrysalis! Come and see it!"

The girls raced over to their classroom.

3

The butterfly was opening and shutting its beautiful black and orange wings.

"Will it fly away now?" said Katie.

"Yes," said Miss Park.
"Your butterfly will find a new plant to lay its eggs on."

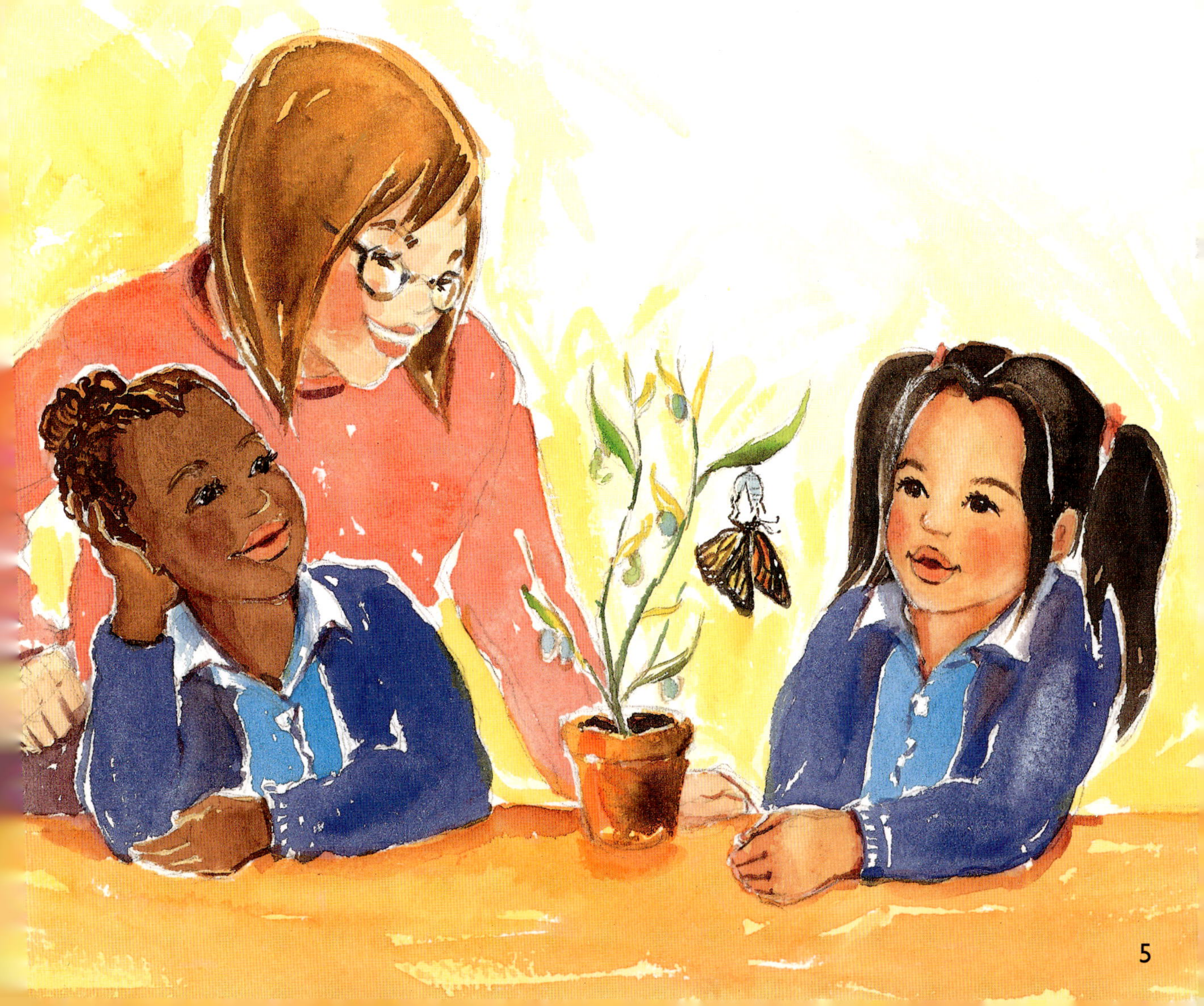

The butterfly moved its wings again.

But it did not fly away.

It started to slip off the chrysalis.

"Oh, no!" cried Anna.

"The butterfly is going to fall."

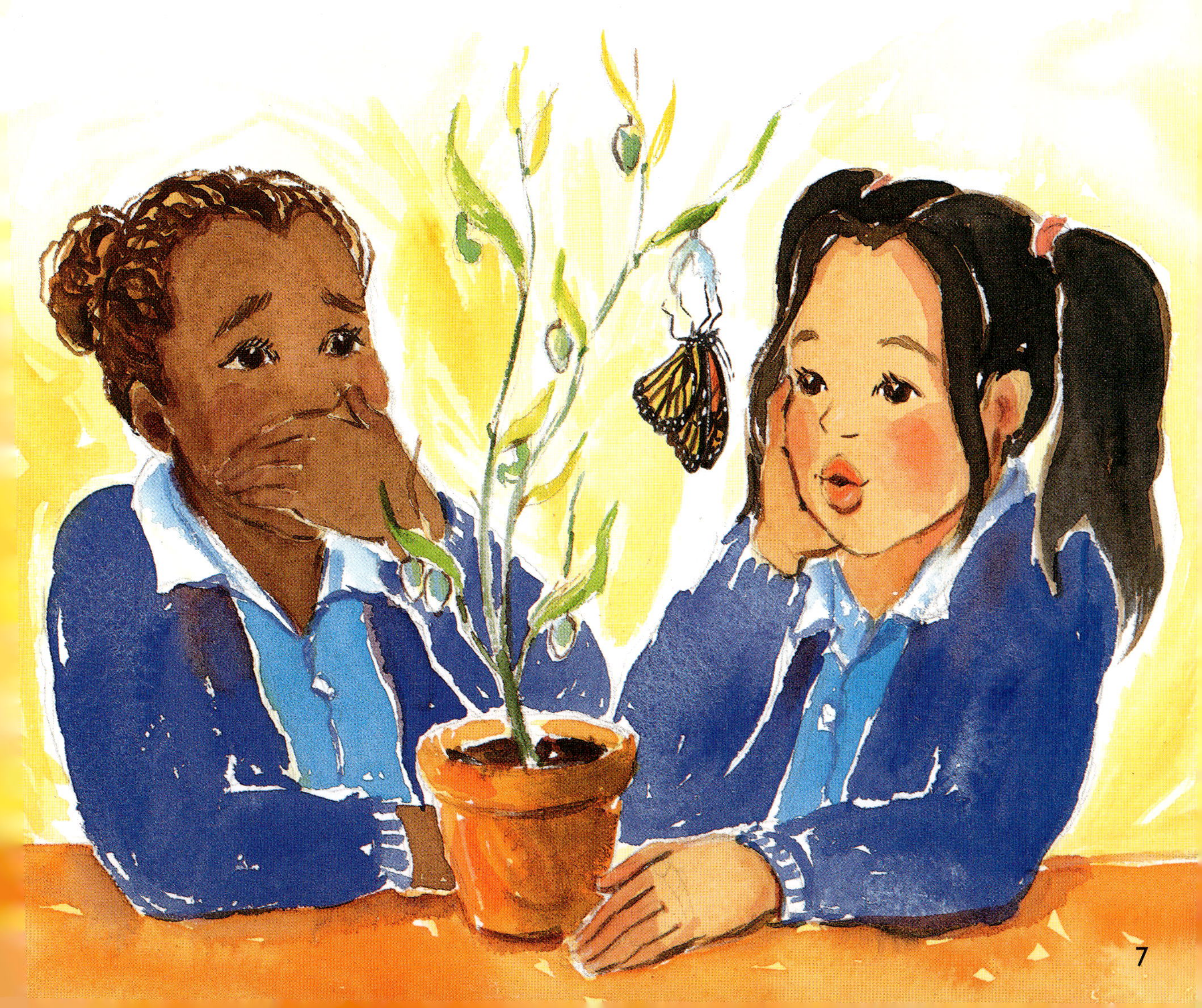

The butterfly fell down
onto Katie's arm, and stayed there.
It opened and shut its wings again.

"It's trying to fly," said Katie.
"I will take it outside."

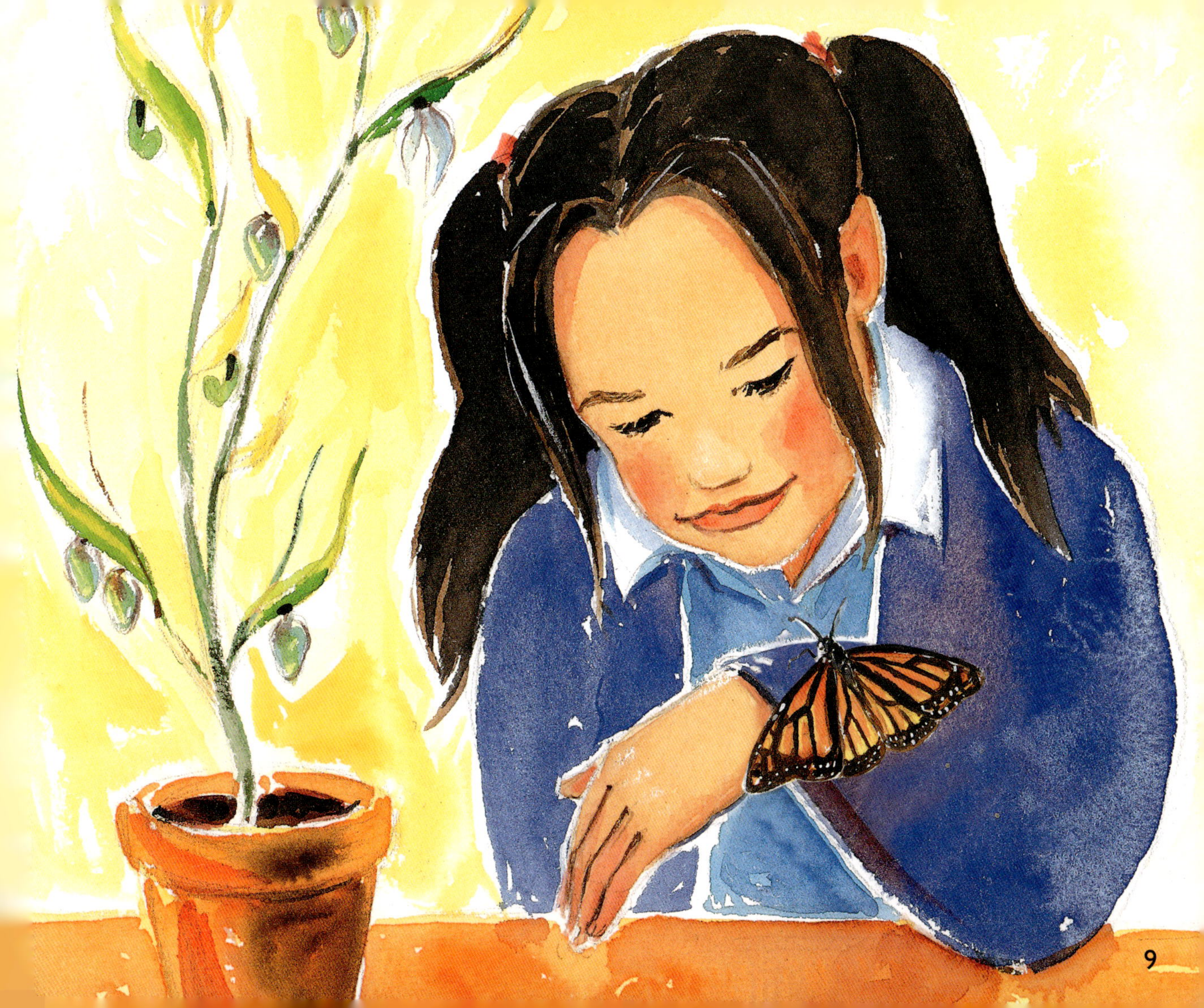

The two girls walked slowly around the playground.

The butterfly did not move. It stayed on Katie's arm.

"What can we do?" said Anna.

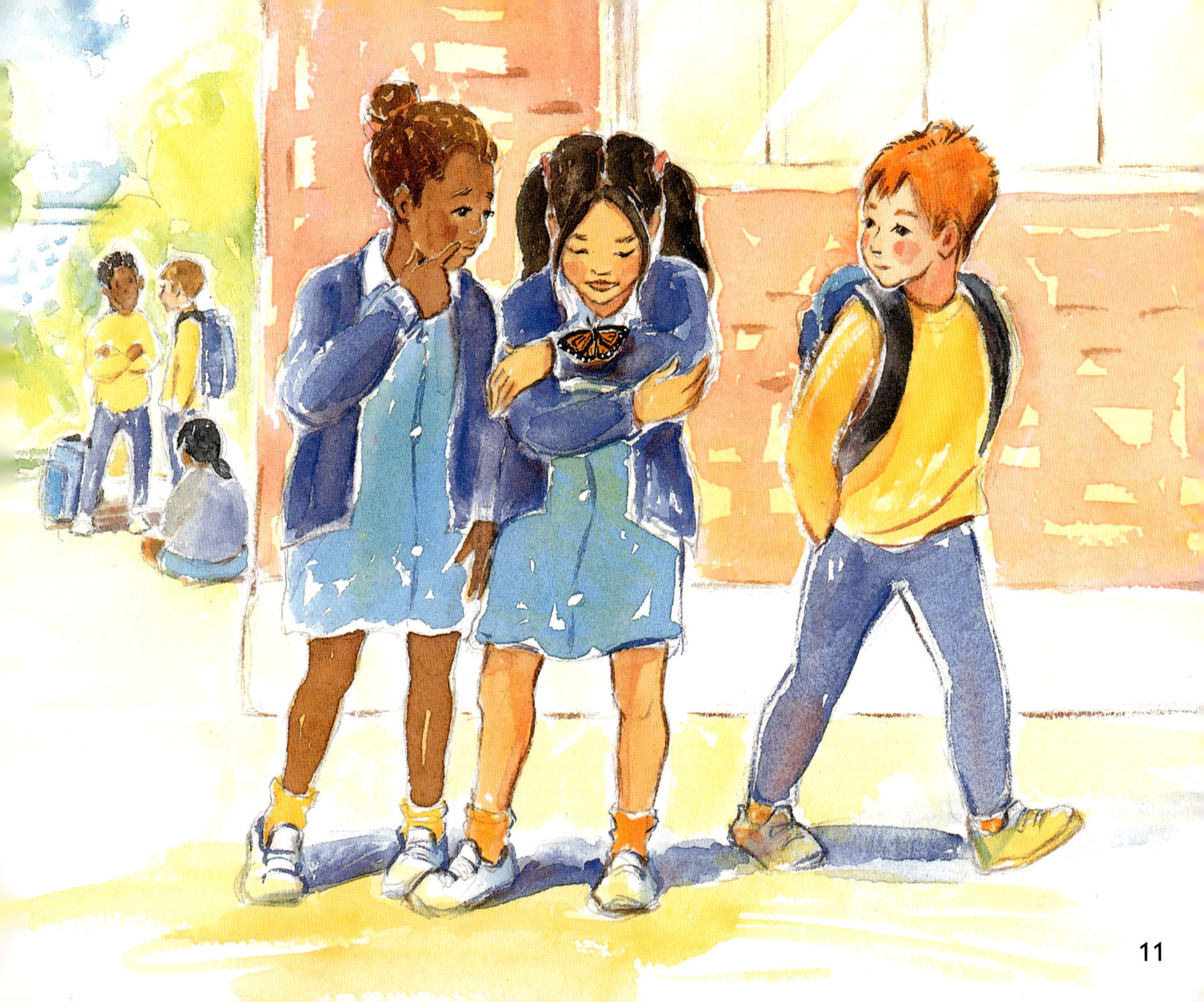

Katie started to run.

The butterfly moved its wings, but it still stayed on her arm.

"It can't fly!" said Anna.

Katie looked at some children who were going down the slide.

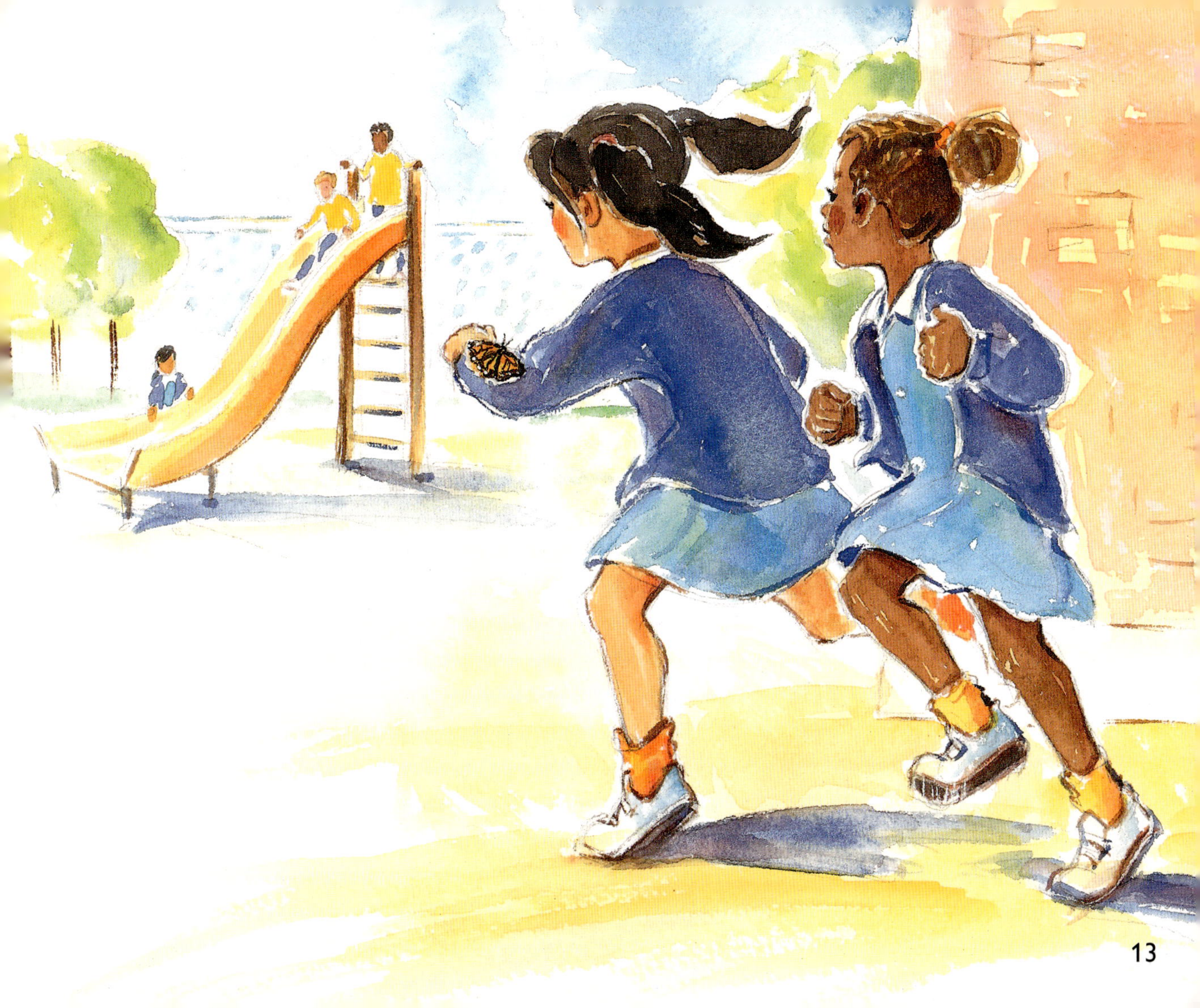

Katie climbed up
to the top of the slide.
Then down she went!

The butterfly opened its wings,
and flew away in the wind.

"There it goes!" cried Anna.

15

"My butterfly **can** fly," said Katie.

"And I helped it!"